PRAISE FOR PIER GIORGIO DI CICCO AND MUNICIPAL MIND

He touches our collective soul and gives us a new language of urban understanding that provides reassurance about the future.

Paul Bedford – Urban Mentor and former Chief Planner, City of Toronto

The wonderful ideas that are in this book about passion and art will swim around in your brain poking at old beliefs and testing core ideas about cherished places, how they work and how they can be catalysts for renewing your neighborhood or even your entire city. GET and READ!

Fred Kent – Principal, Project for Public Spaces, New York

Pier Giorgio Di Cicco is a poet, which makes him the most useful technician of the modern city.

Joe Berridge – Principal, Urban Strategies

Pier Giorgio Di Cicco is a dangerous man. He is dangerous because he dares to speak the truth about the city. Unwilling simply to mouth the pieties of creativity and urban innovation, he argues passionately for the soul of the city, for the integration of art, spirit, and creation in the daily experience of place.

Alan M. Webber – Founding Editor, Fast Company Magazine

There are no gloss-overs in this work, only honest and insightful truths. This is a must read for anyone who wonders about the future of our western civilization.

Jim Dewald – Strategy and Global Management, U. of Calgary

This is a highly motivating flow of inspirations that should be required reading for all who are involved in the creation of environments for living life as it is meant to be.

Frank Nuovo – Designer of the Nokia cellphone, Principle Designer, Vertu

Toronto's Poet Laureate is a treasure and this collection gives the creative city movement both depth and inspiration. It is powerful and I highly recommend it.

Tim Jones – CEO, Artscape

The city that can feel itself through such a poetic vision is a place that is robust enough to become vital and loved and strong enough to survive hate from the uninitiated. A city needs a poet to help the collective perception of itself.

Will Alsop – Architect

His creative city is a work in progress, prompting us to think differently about our city, to dare to be great.

Rita Davies – Executive Director, Toronto Culture Division

... a voice of passion, perception and love who whips our thinking on how to make ours a city of connectivity, kindness and creativity.

Colin Jackson – EPCOR Centre, Calgary, Alberta

This work is a beautifully crafted set of chatauquas that only a philosopher gifted with the power of poetry could deliver. It is an exhortation against the pathology of rules for the sake of control and an impassioned and eloquent plea for embracing the wonder of the random. Required reading for all citizens of the city.

Ted Tyndorf – Chief Planner of the City of Toronto

Pier Giorgio Di Cicco has extended the role of Poet Laureate beyond the area of arts advocacy and into the realm of "civic aesthetic," a term he coined to define building a city through citizenship, civic ethic and urban psychology. His urban philosophy has found popularity in forums ranging from the Prime Minister's Advisory Committee on Cities and Communities and The Creative Cities Project of the Ontario and Toronto governments, to The Waterfront Revitalization Corporation and international conferences on urban sustainability. He is a Roman Catholic Priest, Curator of the Toronto Museum Project and Center for Global Cities and teaches for the Department of Italian Studies at the University of Toronto.

MUNICIPAL MIND

MANIFESTOS
FOR THE CREATIVE CITY

MUNICIPAL MIND

MANIFESTOS
FOR THE CREATIVE CITY

PIER GIORGIO DI CICCO

With an afterword by Charles Landry

MANSFIELD PRESS | CITY BUILDING BOOKS
IN ASSOCIATION WITH COMEDIA
2007

Library and Archives Canada Cataloguing in Publication

Di Cicco, Pier Giorgio, 1949-
    Municipal mind : manifestos for the creative city / Pier
Giorgio Di Cicco.

ISBN 978-1-894469-32-6

    1. Sociology, Urban.   2. Cities and towns – Psychological
aspects. I. Title.

HT153.D49 2007   307.76
C2007-902944-2

Design: Denis De Klerck / Mansfield Creative
Cover Photos: iStockphoto

The publication of Municipal Mind
has been generously supported by
The Canada Council for the Arts and
The Ontario Arts Council.

Mansfield Press Inc.
25 Mansfield Avenue, Toronto, Ontario, Canada M6J 2A9
Publisher: Denis De Klerck
www.mansfieldpress.net

For Toronto – Future of the Global City

*In the city of Brahman is a secret dwelling,
the lotus of the heart. Within this dwelling is a
space, and within that space is the fulfillment
of our desires. What is within that space
should be longed for and realized.*

-CHANDOGYA UPANISHAD

PREFACE

What the world doesn't need is another book about cities. Writing about cities is kind of like writing poetry: most anyone can try their hand at it. Pianists require pianos, artists require canvas, sculptors require a medium. All the poetaster needs is pen and paper, or keyboard and computer chip. But then, one does not need to be a developer, or a planner, or an architect or a statistician to see that the city one lives in is ugly, or beautiful, or lyrical, or uninspiring or seductive to loyalty, or worthy of sentiment. Most anyone can try it, and the newspapers are full of journalists turned city thinkers, and cultural strategists become creative city gurus, or chief planners become urban mentors, and worse – poets practicing urban poetics.

But then, isn't a city a poem in progress? Aren't the citizens the authors of the poem they will have to read to their children? The citizen must self-identify as an artist, with the same moral commitment to ideals, before we can have any credible allegiance to our environment. This is the key to sustainability. Until we see each other, not just as interdependent, but as implicit in each other, we will not be inspired to civic care. Poetic? Holism demands the terms that can seduce us towards it.

Another book about cities. No indices, without footnotes; it doesn't tip its hat to Le Corbusier, or Jane Jacobs, or Lewis Mumford, or Kevin Lynch – to the many pundits of the urban lament, the champions of Oz and the sirens of innovation. We have many manuals of diagnostic planning, with no proactive sense of the civic malaise. This is not a book about how to fix things. This is about exposing what corrupts or excites the urban motive.

This book is a series of manifestos and reflections on what makes up the creative city. It states the obvious, and laments, not that there is no science of the obvious, but that the obvious escapes us as we wait around for verification and empirical charter. The situation is drastic, and the truth startlingly rude. Cities are built by the market, and we stand around with notepads or sullen faces remarking on what could have been done better or might have been done worse. But the damage has already been done. Cities are travesties of construction, and all we can hope to do is to acquire a civic aesthetic that will resurrect us among the tombstones of construction and make the landscape livable by the light of citizenship. If we're lucky, we might even tear things down before we are completely harvested by the scythe of wealth generation.

It isn't so much a failure of the market that accounts for ugly cities; it's more like a failure of heart. And imagination comes from heart. Imagination and commerce have met historically. Imagination and business had known each other, and created the lastingly beautiful in design, configuration, monument and public square; in waterfront and housing, in skyline and neighborhood; those fortunate times when the civic heart flirted with economic interest – when an idea went up, because it was beautiful, and the builders took a few dollars extra to give back to the civic a kiss, as a statement of fidelity to a place of drama, pain and shared sacrifice and expected intimacies called the city. Expedience disguised as modernism obfuscated this arrangement.

This book does more than court the obvious. It prescribes an aesthetic intuited in the heart of the citizen, the desire of the citizen for elements one no longer dares to ask for – conviviality, joy, delight in wonder, the shared forum of imagining and play, of unreserved laughter and serenity – all the fluff things we have decided we have no levers for, but yearn for, all the playful and ecstatic registers that justify city life, without which the city becomes a place of business, or indentured servitude.

Having walked the valley of policy and administration with the strategists of the urban, I have found no index that wasn't a eulogy, a corroboration of the damage after the fact. All the indices in the world will not explain or generate what makes a town alive or dead, anemic or robust, hopeful or self-destructive. It is not unlike the mystery of what keeps a person hopeful and idealistic. There may be an unmanufacturable thing called "an appetite for life" without which a city cannot move ahead; we may be quick to call a town that knows prosperity "creative," but a town that has no appetite for life is not a great town, nor a livable town, nor a sustainable town, much less creative. For the appetite for life is immeasurable except by the most obvious proprioceptors, our senses, our intuitions, our gut instincts. And the gusto for life is evident or isn't, by our faces, our bodies, our relaxation in our bodies, our ability to choreograph our day into the joyous encounter with others. You won't find stats to replace a sense of a town being hostile or friendly, joyous or glum, hospitable or wary. Finally all our judgments of a city boil down to feelings. Until we see feelings as the quick deductions of reason, we will not trust ourselves to build cities well. Indices and figures will only corroborate what our feelings already told us: that a town was hospitable or hostile, rich in hope or hopeless, worthy of inhabited feeling, or busy, but dis-inhabited by its citizens. The empirical mop-up won't redress the question of why we misread our feelings in the first place, or why we lacked the heart to confront the architecture of the space between people.

This book is not about what can be done better, but what we cannot do without. It suggests that diagnosing a city by its construction is like treating the symptoms of a disease. It says nothing about the cause. The cause of the disease is what one finally wants to root out – and the cause is not to be found in bad planning, or good planning, in better allocation of capital funding or public money or private sector initiative. The cause of the disease is not to be found in the debate between schools of aesthetic, or schools of thought.

The cause of urban illness or the health of urban serenity is to be found in the relationship between primal human desires and the construction that mirrors them or stunts them. Where there is a disconnect between the civic dream and the market hunger, there is an area called the creative city that rejoins the project of dreaming and the project of building. There is at the centre of the urban discussion a realm called "civic aesthetic," where the city must be re-aligned to the dreams of citizens and where the building, is measured in compliance with, or by transgression of, the civic dream.

This book is a series of manifestos for the rehabilitation of that dream.

CREATIVE MANIFESTO

A city is not happy owing just to prosperity or economic opportunity. It is happy in the hope and business of human and meaningful things in all spheres of endeavor. Art is about highlighting every sphere of endeavor, until the "artistic" is seen as a way of life, not just something formalized on the page, on the screen, on the stage. A vibrant urban art teaches the art of life; but if the daily life is not artistic, inspired by intimacy, zest and sociality, the passion is missing, and a city without passion is just a city of artistic events.

The purpose of the arts in a city is to make a city fall in love with itself. Such a city knows passion as its source. It takes joy in seeing what it has made, with the urge to regenerate that joy in an atmosphere of risk, adventure and trust. This requires of a city an ability to rejoice beyond the point of pride. However much a city prides itself in plans and accomplishments, the congratulations must become rejoicings that spark the impulse to create again and again without cowering under the restraints of conservatism, "correctness" or globalization. What is required is an essential atmosphere of passion. Without it, a city puts up bad buildings, invents bandage solutions, and claims merely a topology of artistic events cosmetic to daily life.

What are the strategies? Our cities are fond of the implementation of "zero tolerance" for just about any form of abuse. They would do well to exercise zero tolerance for that which enfeebles the passionate imagination of a city. What enfeebles it?

> The notion that money predicates vision.
> The mean-spiritedness that criticizes before it allows.

The conventions of "safeness" from either the left or the right.
Anything that discourages human encounter in the interest of expedience and time-saving.

These elements are at the root of cultural anemia. To discourage them is to begin to create a new attitude. You can't enforce an attitude. Neither can you legislate the human heart. You can, however, inspire it by an example of passion and risk-taking, in an atmosphere in which passion and risk-taking can take place. This is the job of the city at large, to understand that passion and risk begin in daily encounter, on the canvas of everyday life. At the same time a city's art must give the impression that art is as indispensable a thing as water, or food – elementary and elemental to the quality of life. A great city knows this, at the core. It does not see art as adjacent, peripheral or supplementary, and so the lines between business and culture break down and all activities are informed by a spirit of adventure and creativity, and commerce and culture cease to be opposites. A true creative city must look glamorous to itself. By glamour I mean a city's attraction to it's own uniqueness, moved by the conviction that there is a style of creativity that can only be done there. A city must believe this. Artists and citizens must believe this, and when they do, the artist and citizen become one. When the artist and citizen become one, an ethos is created, and art becomes the signature of that ethos.

WHAT A MUNICIPALITY OWES ITS CITIZENS

Each new municipal administration owes its citizens the legacy of an idea that resonates before and after the clang of turnstiles, well after the excitement of premieres and the carousel of artistic events. An idea that translates as the hope each citizen has for a civic landscape that inspires closeness, and not mere connectedness; an idea that improvises civic enthusiasm and is served by a municipal policy that furthers that enthusiasm.

True creative cities produce the legacy of an idea that does what funding cannot do: to foster the incentive to create again and again as a spontaneous civic gesture of expression. Such an impulse, self-renewing, joyous and contagious, inevitably induces prosperity, because it charms both citizen and visitor. This charism is at the heart of the creative city.

"Destination points" (museums, monuments, galleries) are incidental to the real reason people go to Paris, London, New York, and assorted glamourous spots. People go to great cities to "catch" the buzz, the electric feel incidentally ambered in galleries, institutions and archives. Vibrancy emanates from the heart of the city — better known as Montmartre than the Louvre, better known as Greenwich Village than the Metropolitan Opera, better known as Soho than the National Theatre. Showcase is the silhouette of cultural soul. Cities are loved, not for "official" art, but because that art alludes to a treasure alchemized within the city's daily life. It is that electricity that the visitor hopes will "rub off." It is not a pilgrimage to official art that draws the pilgrim of art. It is an atmosphere of creativity surrounding it. This is central to a city that is both attractive and self-attracting.

A city's greatness is manifest in a people confident in their ability to take risks, to encounter, share with each other, speak with each other, in the casual grace of citizens who are not self-conscious of norms and predictability.

City thinkers become artists when they leave behind the legacy of an idea that reverberates in the civic heart and leaves the citizen with a hunger to make an art of the city.

It is this spirit that moves the mind to construct. Without this premise, city-building is crippled. "Construction" without the foundation of passionate spirit is no legacy at all.

WHAT DOES LOVE HAVE TO DO WITH IT?

When one falls in love, one becomes credible; so it is with a city when it falls in love with itself. It becomes credible, believable to itself. And it attracts. When civic leaders are in love with their cities they are listened to; they are credible. People know this: that the quality of life is initially and inevitably predicated by love. And prescriptions not fired by the passion for a town are useless. You cannot fool the instinct of people, all of whom recognize what they themselves aspire to – a passion for what is at stake. And what is at stake is always the quality of life, which people know cannot be bettered, unless love is factored in.

People who are not in love are irresponsible. A town that is not in love with itself is irresponsible, and civically apt for mistakes. Responsibility is a cold duty. It inspires no one. A citizenry is incited to action by the eros of mutual care, by having a common object of love – their city. A town that is not in love will cut corners; lose sight of the common good. It loses sight of the common good because it has lost sight of what is commonly beautiful, and the beautiful is not landscape, or cityscape or architectonic; the beautiful is what people have built in the spaces between each other – a reciprocity, an exchange of ideals and a shared vision.

HOW THE CREATIVE CITY BEHAVES

A city must have a literacy of grace before it can have a literacy of invention. A literacy of grace is the ability to recognize and transact the everyday by the terms of civic mutuality and generosity. The graceful interchange of citizens precludes the graceful exchange of ideas. This grace combines a confidence and a civic ease and departs from more than a project of self-esteem. A healthy city is inspired by a heritage of struggle, sacrifice, and hope and is not forever at the reconstruction of its ego. It does not sally into civic initiative by increments and by always checking its pulse. It is courageous by forgetting itself and assuming the best in civic motive and presuming a common appetite for excellence. And the dynamisms of mere transaction will not do to motivate citizens to collaborative work. Creativity is not negotiated exchange. It is the spontaneous and courageous self-giving of creative urge that trusts in reciprocity, but doesn't wait for reciprocity.

Creativity is stunted by political correctness. It looks for the generosity of self-giving without the oppressive tabulations of risk management.

TRUE CULTURAL STEWARDSHIP

A creative municipality discourages the political correctness that keeps the citizen from forms of play and curiosity, exploration and adventure. The creative municipality takes on the psychology of creativity. Culture managers must know when to drop the terms of discourse and facilitate the creative phenomenon with language that appeals to the heart and the imagination. The creative heart seeks the vocabulary of empathy, compassion and cohabitation, not the abstractions of flow charts and the metaphors of "project management." Good cultural stewardship recognizes that culture strategy is an art and knows that the best strategy is sometimes just to get out of the way.

Cultural stewardship cultivates patience and humility for the mystery that sustains creativity. We do not manage the abundance of the gift. Creativity commands our allegiance, and we do not command it. This humility helps us plan with care and sensitivity, helps us cherish the wisdom not to barge in where the alchemy of imagining has barely begun. Good city-building calls for the same artfulness. Meditation on the city helps us to see the whole, to reflect on its needs in a dialogue of civic request; it gives cities time to dress themselves well as works of art without attending to the curfews of economic dread. It is good to not fear that investment will run off in other directions while the insights are gradually schooled by civic needs and requests for the beautiful. It is good not to confuse project with the natural enthusiasms that build a city in a casual pace of affection.

CULTURE AND POLICY

Culture discussions take into account sociology, economics, multiculturalism, demographics, the arts, systems analysis, but, strangely, not civic psychology. It is assumed that people want what we have heard they want, what we imagine they might want, what we imagine we should want (e.g. diversity, inclusion, the creative market place, a global economy, an aggressive technology). It is not that these things are not useful as public levers for market and ideology. However, policy thinkers mistakenly discount the ambivalences in civic psychology.

Every public virtue must leave private room to wonder. It is in this critical ambiguity that authentic public values are shaped. For example: "diversity" might well contradict the contemporary need for self-referencing; or the notion of "inclusion" may not find its opposite in "exclusion" but in the psychic space the individual needs to subsist in dense environments. For that matter, "a creative market place" may defy the plain intuition that market and creativity don't go together (though they profitably might). A "global economy" may be touted as dire reality, yet appear to the citizen as a desertion of local autonomy. New technology, however useful, may be resented in its very inevitability.

Ambivalences are significant, and human. Where they are ignored in policy discussion, policy discussion ends up ignoring popular resentment. And it is a mistake to think that popular resentment always finds a voice, or a lobby or ombudsman. More often than not popular resentment ends up as private resistance. And this resistance will not enter the forum of creativity.

Weaving a creative civic and national fabric calls for amenability in the public and private mind. It cannot be merely assumed that citizens are free to choose the glamorized versions of publicly commended goals, much less what branding commends. Creativity does not begin with the goals. It begins in the uninhibited psychology that does not feel "led" by the consensus, but is drawn to the consensus, only when it is "invited" to the official ideals, and not "rallied" to the official ideals.

HOW THE MUNICIPALITY
ENCOURAGES CREATIVITY

Creativity ventures into hospitality, not into urban deserts of anxiety and protocol. Accountability, hysterical response to crisis, the culture of fear fuelled by the media, the assiduous witch hunts for the dishonesties of the small minded, obsession with the vagaries of human weakness – these rob the civic of its willingness to play, discover and experiment. Municipal anxiety stunts civic generosity. And ordering the civic heart by regulation and by-law consciousness will not set the stage for casual good will. When regulation seeks to eliminate the happenstance nature of life, spontaneity is held hostage and creativity becomes an abstraction. A city obsessed with protocol will not have creative citizens, diverse or otherwise.

The global strategy for the management of billions of people amounts to a strategy of policing and regulation, calculation and control. It is the corporate answer to diversity, divergent interests and fractal ideologies. The "corporate" is concerned with minimizing friction, by all appearances for the good of all, by the neutralizing tactics of political correctness and the mood valves of global media. The global-corporate solution is about charting the weather of consumer trends in the context of harvesting human labour. There is no heart in the multi-nationals for the project of finding out what holds people together in a civic vision.

The creative city retaliates against the brute strategies of globalization, by ensuring that the ethic of governance highlights a code of common humanity. It designs streets and buildings that inspire encounter. It lets go of unreasonable circumspections in its services and enforcements. It replaces an ethic of boundary and protocol with an ethic of welcome and response. The style of municipal action itself must imitate the dynamic of creativity, – benevolent intelligence with a regard for allowance and response. In such a way, the city is not propelled merely by market agendas. It creates an ambience in which productivity amounts to the volunteerism of civic invention. This civic invention is enabled by a code of allowance and response.

The ethic of welcome and response must be the tacit ethic of any metropolis that would see its economy prosper by creativity; and the strategies for disseminating such a creative ethic do not begin with the arts. They begin with campaigns of encouragement among citizens themselves, aided by the marketing, communications and example of the municipality that implicitly assumes and explicitly proclaims the ethic of welcome and response.

CIVIC ENGAGEMENT AND CREATIVITY

The urban challenge is not about the "interaction" of citizens but the involvement of citizens. People "involved" with each other come away with something of each other. When they "interact" they come away with little more than was invested. Interaction is the coordination of self through others, not the extending of self by risk.

The ethic of civil behaviouralism requires "involvement." It hones the skills of care and concern, initiates the art of the civic. For it is from compassion, not civic duty, that a city learns to fall in love with itself.

In the secular arena it is never a duty to care compassionately for neighbor and stranger. Yet it is only from involvement and compassion, that the mechanism of passion structures itself. A city that would be passionate must know compassion first, by involvement, and by breaking free of the caveats and procedures that negotiate the private self.

THE URBAN MOTIVE

A creative city motivates a citizenry to a humane reflection on itself by looking, speaking, engaging freely. It requires the rehabilitation of trust. Trust is everyday eroded by media alarms of abuse and danger that exhort us to exercise caution. Distrust is further abetted by the distancing conventions of telecommunications. Technologies that proposed to bring people closer have become the surrogate means of encounter. The body is hijacked on virtual freeways that traffic supply and demand with diminishing need of somatic expression. Chat rooms, on-line buying, on-line services, video games, etc. induce the physical "solitary." We imagine that art will rupture this isolation. But the paradox remains. World technology conspires to disembody the citizens of a city, while a city is compelled to consume virtual technology to compete in the world.

Culture builders try not to look at this paradox "straight-on." They can do little about the supplanting of the physical by virtual technology. More and more money is sunk into the arts as if to create a sandbar between the tides of the "informational," and the disappearing coastline of human intimacy.

Alternately, we try to persuade the commercial sector to employ aesthetics that speak to the "sensual" of a city. The leverage here is that it is good for business to re-address the somatic and aesthetic requirements of citizens. This is the tired forum of "creativity and business"; a dialogue that attempts to put the paradox to sleep by making a city look "artsy." This reasoning hopes to neutralize the tension between the local and the global, the personal and the impersonal. This may work, assuming we are not just putting art at the service of industry with the easy thought that what is good for the economy is good for art, and vice-versa. For this kind of thinking only continues to polarize commerce and art, and calls them to negotiate, not join.

Are the commercial requirements of a city to compete in a globalized economy inimical to the call of a civic aesthetic? Culture planners must differentiate between strategies and bandage solutions. A bench at the foot of corporate towers, a park swarmed by skyscrapers, an abstract sculpture protruding at a commercial intersection – these things do not successfully negotiate a civic aesthetic. The citizen cannot be fooled to the artistic by the painting of silos and the converting of warehouses into art-space, or transforming industrial parks into theme-sites.

Where public art in public space is concerned, an axiom might be considered: visual distraction only goes so far so long as people are distracted from each other. We must devise civic strategies that discourage people from being distracted from each other. (Keeping in mind that reconstructing the space between people is never a physical project; it is a metaphysical project, and even a spiritual project).

OUT OF THE SILOS

The cultural problem in major cities is neither the absence of goodwill for the arts, nor the lack of funding for the arts. The event landscape of most cities is rich, and growing richer. The problem is how to let art spill over into the creative potential of the city at large, in commerce and routine, in business and community.

It is laborious and inefficient to stitch creativity to the fabric of society. It is more intelligent to suppose that creativity is, after all, "renewable energy." It accomplishes itself, regenerates itself if its source is acknowledged, and that source is always the civic heart.

How does a municipality drum culture out of its "sectors"? Energy is not generated with trumpetings of tolerance, diversity, or mere exhortations to creativity. Mandates try to strategize passion, but can't produce it. Passion is desire. Desire is not awakened by mandate or "prescripts." Desire is the self-willed attraction to the marvel of creating. The creative act lures the imagination and the imagination is, in turn, released; not by exhortation and mandate, not by an atmosphere of correction, political or procedural, but by inter-play and play in an atmosphere of civic affection. Prescripts of tolerance, diversity and creativity cannot fire the human heart. They are intellectualisms. They are the tracings of ideas masquerading as joy.

RECOGNIZING CREATIVITY

Joy is the raison d'être of the creative act; the prospect of bringing into the light of day that which was inchoate and formless; the prospect of bringing to common celebration what was inherent in common hopes, the joy of articulating a private dream that turned out to be a public vision. And simply the delight of having conjured the new under the auspices of the communal. Joy is how creativity justifies itself. It is that profoundest of sentiments that all other terms aspire to. Joy is the civic hallmark of a livable and competitive city. Its absence amounts to a city's shameful deficit, or its surrender to the dispiriting forces of the corporational.

The joy of creativity enthuses. It affects and effects. "Effect" is the outward sign of the impact of creative relationship. "Affect" is inter-subjective. Joy is recognized, reciprocated and moves from citizen to citizen, axiomatically; it comes of the need to create, the need to meditate on the features of what is collectively accomplished, to contribute to a consort of novel invention, to be appreciated as an "existential" called the civic. The dream of the civic is not to be separate from the civic body, but to be acknowledgement of it. Such alchemy looks to the city for affirmation and imaging. And the city must not reply with an industry of limitations. Protocol, boundary consciousness and political correctness seek to nurture the alchemy of creating, but in fact stunt it. They do not provide the atmosphere for passion, but merely a containment for it. "Containment," in both spirit and ethic, is what enfeebles a city's culture.

The joy of creating happens naturally and spontaneously. It is often our arrogance to usher it, facilitate it and strategize it. Creativity manages itself in the home, on the canvas, on the street. The joy of creating knows no forum. The task of culture planning is not to provide a forum, but to unimpede the flow of creative "affect." The "affect" is what touches the "other" – the neighbor, the colleague, the citizen, having enlivened the one creating. Creativity animates the natural enthusiasm of the creative person. This enthusiasm can be met, either by an ethic of welcome and response; or by an ethic of boundary and protocol. The ethic of boundary and protocol corrupts the urban nature. It is the predisposition of our times, a pre-disposition that impedes the flow of creative enthusiasm, person to person. It is a consciousness that renders each creative sector discrete, and keeps discrete the events of art in every sector of daily life.

Creativity, then, does not take well to uninspired help. It hunts its own game. It manifests and invites joy. It asks only for a climate of trust and allowance. The business of governance is more properly to remove that which debilitates the creative will. The municipal tends to debilitate by bureaucratic circumspection, by the conscription to fiscal convenience, by the willful compliance to market agendas, by settling for the mediocre when the extraordinary seems hazardous. Such a municipality does not trust its citizens by their enthusiasms. It trusts in their greed and uncertainty. Such an ethic does not inspire a citizenry to creativity.

A city welcomes the creative, not just by fostering or funding, but by inviting the intelligence of the creative, and styling itself after it. A conspicuous project of creativity, too, will defeat the creative agenda. The rallying of creativity produces mere invention. The allowance of creativity produces radical thinking. Radical thinking occurs where psychology is disposed to possibility. Human psychology, left to itself, will re-originate and share. It finds its way to innovation, if not badgered by regimen and expedience.

And governance must participate in that psychology. Creativity moves by the casual endorsement of its own enthusiasm. With subtlety and with this enthusiasm, creativity permeates industry and all sectors. It becomes the spirit of a city and a way of life.

In this way creativity shapes the city, while the city formalizes a climate conducive to it.

SELF CONSCIOUSNESS: THE ENEMY
OF THE CREATIVE CITY

If a city is self-conscious (sensitive to its physical and exterior demeanor in a way that is inhibitory to response) – it cannot unlock its creative potential. If appearance and concern about the outcome of the gesturals of interaction come before spontaneity and unfettered risk-taking, the city is handicapped in its planning and services in the area of creativity.

There must be vigilance about the programs, prescripts and bylaws that intimidate the civic body and inhibit its expression as a medium for healthy citizenship. It's not a case of simply relaxing social norms, or of inducement to greater self-expression, or such clichés. It is about restoring to the urban citizen the body that is the reflexive mediator of passion. The freedom to explore a park or a public space designed for the body as venue for encounter cannot be contradicted with foolish bylaws and caveats to participation. There is no point to landscaping a public park if there is a sign that reads "Park closes at 11 pm." There's no point to public festivals and civic events if the parking police are out in droves making the most of civic oversight. There is no point to well designed city paths if gatherings are seen as a public nuisance. And the remedy is not as simple as distinguishing between necessary policing and over-policing. The municipal thinking must be on guard against a regulatory ethic that establishes norms contrary to the philosophy of public space. Public space in theory invites exploration, encounter and activity, but municipal and corporate thinking can over-regulate it, limit it, and even extinguish it.

Where there is excessive rule-consciousness, the citizen is inhibited and banished from the public forum, and discouraged from the free play of creativity. Ingenious design cannot redress the contradictions of bylaw and injunction. This rule-consciousness is anathema to the creative city. It must be detected and remedied. It keeps the passion of a city at arms-length, always.

37

THE CREATIVE CITY IS THE PASSIONATE CITY

The creative city understands passion as more than a debate about notions of "buzz," "excitement," "cool," "hip," etc. Such elements are functions of passion, not to be confused with passion itself. Relieve "passion" of its pop evocations and one finds it as native and central to the civic psychology. Passion is the style of energy with which a citizenry responds to the marvelous or the terrible, to crisis or cooperation, to adversity or constraint. It is the degree to which a citizenry embraces delight. It amounts to a gusto for life, an appetite for it, and it is not easily mustered up by slogans and it is not easily abashed by intimidation or circumspection. Passion is the zeal with which one responds to the invitation to create. Passion is the degree of energism that people bring to bear on events in a way that either negates life or encourages life. Passion mobilizes civic will. Schemes for creativity amount to nothing, if the mechanism for passion isn't strengthened in the body politic. Passion is a muscularity that the civic psychology must have; it is the genesis of response to creative invitation. Passion is only awakened by the "eros" of idea, possibility or vision. Eros is the sensual mentation of the beautiful. When an idea is lovely, the creative will is impassioned.

PASSION AND THE PHYSICAL CITY

A creative city then, lives in an ethos of responsiveness. The appetite for life has to be there, freed of the wastage of cynicism, freed of the constraints and caveats that a hyper-regulated metropolis offers, freed of the endless sanctions and provisos against physical encounter. For physical encounter is the first and final meeting place of art and mind, body and soul.

Passion begins with the body, is expressed by the body, finds its apotheosis by the body. The body is the mediator of civic life. The body is the heir to the city as sacred place. Architecture gives forum to the body's expression. It is the art that instructs people in how to use their bodies as mediums of deeper engagement. Urban design seeks to give the body a confluence by graceful skylines, easeful pathways, public spaces, meditations of space that develop into the syntax of encounter. It is the body, and the happiness of the body that the city provides furniture for, creates walking spaces for, provides shelter for, provides recreation for. And the spirit that cannot access physical expression, cannot release true passion. The extent to which the city conditions the civic body to inhibition, is the measure to which a city extinguishes its passion. Such a city cannot hope to excite by an idea or civic design.

You can judge a city firstly and mainly by the interaction of bodies, exchanges of social negotiation that are somatic, verbal and visual and physical. Contact cannot be an abstraction, least of all in a time when the violation of public space is seen as an affront to personal space. You can have a "safe" city, but at the risk of having a nonphysical city. A city that is not manifest in physical, verbal and sensory self-involvement, a citizenry that does not involve itself with the "senses" of others cannot know the city as a creative habitat, for it is self-conscious. And self-consciousness is the enemy of passion. The first and most visible index of the health of a city, the hardest thing to quantify and the easiest thing to diagnose is its self-consciousness. It is evident, by degrees, in every city. Where there is much of it, the city goes about its business, and is satisfied with that. And where there is less of it, a city is robust and free to venture, free to re-imagine itself.

THE PRIVATE SELF VERSUS THE CREATIVE CITY

There is a paradox in the civic nature. The citizen resents densification, yet wants to be seduced to public encounter. Our public lives have become "negotiations," and our private lives have become things to usher carefully into the public sphere. The public sphere is scripted by cynicism in an era of breeched trust, in a landscape of discredited institutions, until there is finally a dogged surrender to the global zeitgeist of self-interest. In such a setting, the private self is bound to be aggrandized and cherished. The private self is the child in us that seeks protection, that space in which we devise our defense against complexity, that space which houses our nerve zones of skepticism, alerting us to what is familiar and to what is foreign. It is the space we carefully renegotiate and defend with virtuality. The private self is nemesis of the city and is threatened by the city, though it uses the city to hide in, by the containment of self in condos, by the protection of self by boundary laws, bylaws, gated communities, ordinances and privacy laws. In such a setting individual rights are recruited to the maintenance of the domain of the private self. Human rights become an appeal to a legislative rationale for justifying the "solitary." Though the individual does not always wish to be solitary, the private self builds a city that ensures the solitary.

It is a mixed message that individuals give themselves in today's urban world. The public and the private are oppositional and consequently, public space and private space are in opposition. And negotiation is the sad arbiter of both. Negotiation replaces the graceful movement from public to private and back again, the art of which belongs to the citizen and begins in the citizen. The tension between public space and private space cannot be reconciled by urban design or policy, until the citizen configures these contradictory desires, and makes an art of their apparent paradox.

THE NATURE OF CREATIVITY

Creativity is not the rare gift of the artist, or the poet. It is what calls a human being to author his or her life by the creation of cities, families, communities. It is that identifier in each person that cries out for authentication. It is that dormant genius, which, if suppressed, finds release in bombings, mental unhealth and crime. This is the reality that global strategy must understand, independent of creativity as a lever to economy, or the vanity of the sovereign.

Today's call to be creative is ceaseless. But people will resist conscription above and beyond the tasks of consciousness-raising and the agendas of awareness homilized by pop morality. Prescribed aspiration has reached critical mass. Only impassioned beliefs will persuade. Cynicism is too widespread for just another "good idea." The best notions are added to the list of suspect agendas. People are happy to pay lip service to a trend; but creativity is what they keep to themselves away from the jaws of market hunger. Citizens guard their creativity jealously. They know it has very much to do with their "soul." They'll surrender long hours and application to the economic engines that sustain them, but they won't casually yield the play, spontaneity and trust that companion creativity. They detect the market motive behind the trend. If the "creative city" looks like a trend, or just another means of exploiting human capital, it won't get the pledge of imagination. You cannot fool people into surrendering their most precious of personal resources – creativity.

Creativity knows no clocks, timetables, or flow-charts. It is that space where people re-invent the world, in the time that is stolen from the world, where they can be themselves and think imaginatively. People want to "relax" into their skills, and not be herded into the building of cultural pyramids. For creative skills are not commodities and currencies of exchange. They are the thumbprints of personal identity and the styles of individuation. To respect this is to persuade people to creativity.

The global intelligence would like to harvest creativity, without understanding that it stems from a mystery, an unfathomable resource that will either yield its graces or give us as little as we ask in the name of economy.

THE ARTISTIC CAVEAT

The artist knows that failure is the rubric of success, that there is no waste in the economy of creation. Anything not used finds its place, sooner or later. The artist knows that, in creating, to quote W. B. Yeats, "one is wrestling with a god." Such is creativity. One is not wrestling with one's abilities, ambitions or limitations. Those may be transcended with the grace to engage with the unknown.

In the world of creativity, it is the vision that has you on the leash, not the other way around. The vision won't behave as neatly as numbers on a ledger. And application is no guarantee in the business of creation. Application is just the entry fee that vision demands, along with the courage to "surrender" to insight. One must subscribe to the faith that what was not clear today will be clear tomorrow. The artist knows that to court either the muse or the mother of invention is to learn humility and patience.

It is this ability to not jump the gun, and not force the hand of illumination, that distinguishes the visionary from the professional, the hack from the inspired writer, the greedy developer from a great planner, a leader from a politician. It is what distinguishes a "vibrant" city from a merely "developed" one. A city that has taken time to dress itself well is aware of itself as a work of art, and is beautiful to its citizens.

Creative economies seek invention and innovation. These require mere imagination. We can put them under the banner of creativity and short-change ourselves and our potential as city-builders. Creativity is a way of life. Invention, innovation are the quick harvest; they call for cleverness in negotiating new-level growth. Invention and innovation are the stuff of progress, but not the life-blood of creativity. Creativity hunts a vision. "Progress" is pedantic. Creativity owns imagination. It commands the allegiance and love of the creative person as a way of being. The imagination that comes of that allegiance is powerful, self-renewing, and tireless in its transformations. It permeates all aspects of civic life. It is the only limitless resource.

To know this is to release an industry in perpetual motion. The ethos of creativity, left unchecked, by its natural genius, instructs all witnesses to the shared project of wonder. This is what makes a city great and a society productive.

THE DESIGN OF CREATIVE CITIES

Urban design is the most kinesthetic of all the arts. There is no "watching," or reading, or listening, or being just a spectator in the art of urban design. The citizen "becomes" the art, walks through it, lives in it – completes the art, as the lover for which the design was intended. And the design must love the citizen. The only way the citizen believes the design is by an intuition that the intent and vision was a romance intended for him.

This is where the romance of a city begins; in the assurance that one's bones and conversation, one's voice and acoustic, one's sense of play, visual and purposed, has found its proper forum in whatever building and scenario the city offers. This is the beautiful – to feel invited and to be willing to surrender one's physicality to what is graceful and good, because it does not resist human dimension, but gives it new horizons within the scope of the familiar.

There is one essential philosophical criteria for urban design, and it is the notion of "welcome" – the notion that a design welcomes its inhabitant or visitor, through the strange alchemy of imagination and benevolence, through a sense of generosity in the spirit of the artist. Perhaps because the architect loves the citizen.

This is crucial, not just as a principle of design, but as a corroboration of a city's ethic. An ethic of welcome that cannot first be extended to its citizens by architecture cannot be extended to visitors or present a city to the world as an auspicious place. When we feel welcome in our structures, we are at home, at ease and prone to be creative, and that "buzz" of creative and rejoiced ambience is felt, and passed on; and a city that is too big in many ways is then bonded, made to cohere by an atmosphere of conviviality and trust. To be able to entrust one's body to a building, to a street, to a home, is then to be able to entrust oneself to other people, is to be able to entrust oneself to the civic.

DESIGN AND THE CIVIC

Good design, then, inspires trust, because the citizen feels loved. Good house design is about total habitat; body and environment as one organism, educating us in the intersubjective. It requires an ethical intelligence in the architect and the conjoining of information technology, materials, and aspects of construction beyond the notion of what is serviceable. It grafts these elements onto the sensory ecology of humanness. It calls for an understanding of the citizen, an understanding that the citizen needs more than amenities in cookie cutter subdivisions – it needs more than the trick of hidden infrastructures and more than the zoning that segments and at best achieves "mixed use" as lip service to civic integration. To see design as total habitat is to architect a simulacrum of rhythms and energies and musics and movements inherent in the human body and extending to the body politic.

Current language fails us in the holism required of new design. Our language is dipodic, western, Aristotelian. It requires poets, artists, designers that intuit the wholeness requested by the human experience. The project is to have citizens reflected in their environment. In this way the city is reflected in its structures and the schemes for betterment emerge more from harmony than from purposed interest.

We easily intuit the violations of the holistic. We know when harmonies are neglected in the design surrounding us. It takes good sense and a feel for the indices that will never make it to paper. The sadness in the civic mood is in part, caused by the smog, the confused infrastructure, the incoherent skylines, the holocaust of urban sprawl and the acute societal fragmentation that shows itself in the human being seeking to withdraw in the 21st century.

This can be redressed in part by design that loves the citizen. What does it mean to say that design loves the citizen? It means designing with a kind of care that only comes of compassionate imagination. It calls for designer as "empath," imagining what a blind person would need, what an aged person might need, what the designer himself would dream for others. It means reflecting on what makes a person rejoice. It means designing, not just by visuals, but by understanding that smell, touch and movement are only a part of the human sensorium. The synesthesia of design is complex – the movement of a body in consort with visual requests, the sense of lighting that collaborates with movement to turn attention to others, the use of information technology that is prosthetic to human action and not discrete from it, the use of materials that evoke a sense of the natural, the interplay between one house and another as if they were talking to each other. The principle here is that of relationship as opposed to discrete entities – to bring the citizen to a sense of integrated habitat because the aesthetic of design mirrors the aesthetic of ethical reach. This comprises design that loves the citizen and it summons appreciation in the citizen – and helps restore a literacy of grace in the social order.

THE CONVERSATION OF DESIGN ELEMENTS

Urban components should be in conversation with each other. To add to the conversation that is already there: this is the particular genius of planning. Not to eradicate and create the consistent, but to let the elements, already there, speak to each other. And to join in. And the conversation is varied. Buildings and land allude to each other, infrastructure and housing parley to each other. There is even a murmuring; there is a plea and a request for sharing between a grove of pines and a cloverleaf, between telephone lines and storefronts, between power plants and ravines. Nothing is without the natural conviviance that human meaning makes and brings to the unlikely and the apparently unplanned. Landscaping addresses architecture, the choreography of light investigates colour and shape. Routes and paths surprise, or leave a meditation as they weave through hamlet and brownfield. The citizen joins a conversation, not in which elements contradict each other, but in which the eavesdropping lures one's attention and the intense dialogue of formal structures yields to the casual gossip of store, parkette and houses.

The livable city is a conversation that does not bore or shout or offend. The planner, the architect, watches for the conversation that is already there and adds, with respect for proximities and allowances that accrue from the city's growth, without posturing and din. It calls for respect for what history has brought; not formal history but history that looks like disrepair, and is not; respect for time that has left, not scars, but weathering. The new and the old are not categories. Time has left gradations, and the passage of a few years imbues a character on a city, as on a face. Many expressions and countenances come together. Trees, plazas, archways, underpasses, facades; the many shapes and intimations neither flow, nor startle. They are the city, comfortable in time, in which the citizen walks as in a gallery, neither exhausted, nor enervated, nor dumbfounded. It is the city of the everyday, unpretentious and hospitable. It is the city of the everyday, unpretentious and cohabited. For design is the co-habitation of all things.

THE UNPRETENTIOUS CITY

The city must cease acting out of fear that investment will flow elsewhere if it stops coddling developers.

Fred Kent – Project for Public Spaces

Contemporary skylines are in disarray, so many voices, crying for attention, all boasting a privileged statement of ego or greed. They speak plurality, diversity, and the fevered dreams of affluence. They speak the union of vanity and market obsession. Businesses commemorate their egos, indifferent to civic consensus, while city governments seem helpless to curb the developer's appetite (however fortunate in the absence of municipal vision). It is how cities stay solvent. The development adds to the city coffers and the city without vision uses the money to merely bandage infrastructure. The result: solvent cities and ugly landscapes. Everywhere, cranes and bulldozers shriek prosperity to tourists and investors, and the quiet desperation of the citizen perdures – the civic mood downtrodden, and become a casualty of municipal thinking with no aesthetic.

Dispirited by bickering and blatant architectures, the citizen rummages through the city looking for those sights and spaces that reflect a human scale. The citizen finds consolation in the neighborhoods and unpretentious way stations, the abandoned, the undeveloped, the modest, looking for the town that seeks to be adopted before it capitulates to realty. The citizen seeks to adopt those places, spaces and structures that don't declare, or impose – places that enjoin us to remember our limitations even as we re-invent ourselves, places that don't remind us of the ever growing gulf between the rich and the poor, places that don't betray the future by selling out the past. The citizen feels for the city that has fallen between the cracks and has escaped the brute exercise of wealth generation. The inadvertent, the under-planned, the randomly evolving city left to itself – this draws the affection of the civic lover. What appeals in the city is that which doesn't deny the unseemly labour and drama of having been simply human – the city that doesn't mop up after the holy sweat of having forged gracefulness from the dross of human endeavour. In the truly re-vitalized city, the unfashionable architectures of the past are not whitewashed, cosmeticized or concealed. The attractive city is the unassuming city; the casual gesture of a metropolis unashamed of its past and keen to avoid the mistake of pretension.

The unassuming city is anything but mundane. It cherishes its slovenly sacrifices, forgives its historical gaffes. It glosses no narrative and covets no glamour. Its signature is betterment in the style of hope. It doesn't whore itself to the utopian. Its perfection is in the casual redress of its errors with an imagination founded on self-acceptance. Such a city charms and inspires loyalty in the young who wish to meditate on their city, and not have a city held hostage to lifestyles.

The citizen seeks to adopt a city that in confidence and humility asks something of him and surrenders the themes of acquisition. How cruel is the municipal mind that flogs the citizen again with design that teaches competition and not civic grace. The duty of architecture and city design is to speak to the citizen of acceptance and the themes of welcome that put the citizen at ease in aspiration, and not ambition. It is in this way that design instructs the art of life.

A well designed city redresses the wound of inadequacy that the citizen suffers with every market advertisement. It mutes the bellowing of wealth generation and praises the daily heroism of citizens, their courage and humility in everyday life. Such beauty, reflected in a congruent skyline, reminds the citizens of a style of citizenship that is their own.

The beautiful is what speaks not of limitation, but as grace emerging from the constraints of life's fortunes. The beautiful is what reminds the citizen of the poignancy of the human project. A skyline that dares to rise with this understanding is homage to the city.

CITY OF DREAD: DIAGNOSTICS

— The Civic Mood

There is an air of spitefulness in the civic politic. There is a resentment. There is a hostility. There is a grudge, begotten of failed idealisms and defeated patrimony. When belief in the efficacy of human softness went the way of brute realism and positivism, fun left the province of interaction. There is a spite served by proceduralism and calculation, there is a spite that tries to get back at the society that disappointed its hopes. The machines of justice, accountability and rights cannot mend the damage to collective hope. These are the industries of compensation that seek to offset the disenchantment of the civic heart. Holding each other accountable is the inverse pathology of the want for intimacy. It is a spite that explains discourtesy, it is a spite that speaks enslavement to urban regimen, it is a spite heard in the blaring of horns, in vandalism and ethical subterfuge and the accumulation of wealth without need. It is a spite not to be addressed by public art and openings. It is a spite not easily mollified by the surplus of ingenious initiative. It is a spite that will be effaced only by the example of public benevolence. It is a spite that seeks a witness of the good before it can be re-educated to charity.

— Intimacy

Violence is the reaction to loneliness, the absence of collective ideals, the surrender to market pressures and simply the need to make contact with someone. The damage of life, one's own or that of others, is the pathology of absent intimacy.

Intimacy is the primal request of the civic creature. Intimacy is regarded as optional in the planning of cities, structures, organizations. It is left as the prerogative of citizens to seek their own intimacies within available structures, landscapes and opportunities. It is a mistake.

Anonymity, safety and economic expedience are the lynchpins of globalized thinking. Intimacy has been regarded as a decorative and frivolous element. Yet every development that goes up without a parkette, each street without a city bench, each edifice that intimidates the citizen without inviting, every virtualization of human contact, creates an atmosphere, a zone of inaffectivity as anathematic to humans as an atmosphere of hydrocarbons.

Sustainability begins with the ecology of interaction and civic involvement. The wise usage of environment is instructed by the altruism of city living. The purpose of city living is to perfect and rediscover the city as a forum of unexpected intimacies. The project of anonymity is inimical to the scope of intimacy.

– *Gentrification*

Gentrification is the lifestyle apotheosis of globalization. It can be identified as wealth generation by design affiliations and a lifestyle negotiated by market image and negotiated space. Formerly derelict neighborhoods gone the way of sandblasting, surveillance and new urbanism relatively free of crime, poverty and the fracas of the unemployed. It is the sanitized city, not the creative city. Safe, picturesque and adorned neighborhoods connected by mixed-use development. Homes well kept, tidy and nicely landscaped, with hardly anyone on the streets. The advent of city soul is academic to gentrified neighborhoods. Aside from the pretension of nightlife in metropolitan cores, it is in the edge cities and in the suburban archipelagos that the creative agenda is desperately needed. The city is more than its metropolis. The downtown cores will inevitably be "revitalized." The bulk of the population is in new development: affluent, unengaged communities, withered by the weather of political correctness, without strategies for inviting the civic consciousness to encounter.

There is in the contemporary an ethic of disengagement vying with a need for civic encounter. It is not addressed in the urban discussion. The need to negotiate space is in direct opposition to the idea of a city as a place of civic communion. It is the contradiction of our times. Until it is resolved, the question of city soul and livability cannot move forward. Security and civic adventure cannot strike a balance if social engineering has revised human nature to be suspicious of civic nature.

– The Lifestyle Dream

In the city of dread, lifestyles are the new allegiance. The call of lifestyle accounts for migration, emigration, relocation, new location. People choose cities according to the exigencies of their lifestyles. People once chose a town and made concessions to its peculiarities and personality, accommodating their dreams and goals to the indigenous charm of a place and its ethic. We now seek places that accommodate lifestyles; and lifestyles render places redundant. Consumerism, convenience, infrastructural advantage, safety and status are the arbiters of mobility. People do not move into neighborhoods. They move into class patterns. It is not neighborhood that the ratepayer seeks: it is the evocation of neighborhood with the exigencies of the lifestyle dream.

The lifestyle dream: possibility without allegiance, or allegiance only to that which has possibility. Not allegiance to the failed, the attempted, the sacrificial, not affection for the expenditure of commitment. The lifestyle dream is the future, fevered with acquisition and contemptuous of having had less, the anthem of choice, disdainful of the impoverished. The lifestyle dream – entitlement without patience, tolerance without empathy, a constant ovation to progress, and the chastisement of history. The lifestyle dream – "house farms" blessed by a neighborhood watch, local history sandblasted and secured with locks, and a civic mandate to mind your own business.

The freedom to see whom you want to see on your own terms. It is the logic of separation, justified by branding. It is box condos for a culture that prides itself in thinking outside the box. The lifestyle dream – free of identifications; all but one – that of the ethic of globalization – security at all costs, autonomy without detractors, connectedness without intimacy. The lifestyle dream, to worship the ecology of relationship without communion with others.

– *Owing Hope*

Mutually seduced away from commonality, people don't forgive each other the betrayal of civic society. The harshness of life without confluent goals turns everyone survivalist, and each stranger is seen as more puzzle than possibility. Each glance betrays the shame of civic abjuration. Each glance conceals the longing. Each glance speaks the tacit admission to the failed enterprise of neighborhood, each glance is the trace of civic hunger with a loss of heart.

The spite is the outward show of heartbreak. It is the orphaned civic – that which cries to come home and is enraged at the unguiding world and the abandoned posts of leadership and communal care. The spite dresses itself in apathy, proceduralism and objectification. The civic is wounded, and looks for the pledge of commitment among its own, but it cannot volunteer itself without the arbitrary act and witness of benevolence. In the city of dread, each citizen waits and waits for the other, for the legacy of hope, not knowing that hope is what is owed to the other.

RESTORING THE SOUL TO THE CITY

The challenge of the contemporary city is to be international, without letting competition mar its character. But character thrives where it is freely disposed to do so. For all the contemporary lip service to "rights," the global citizen is opting for safety at the cost of civil liberty. There is, in the new civic nature, a need to withdraw. Civic distrust permeates our cities, resulting in an increase in crime, mental unhealth, and violence proportional to the joylessness of the urban. The city has become a forum of distrust.

Creativity is that expression by which the citizen recognizes an "existential" that furthers its destiny through other people. The premise of encounter alone justifies the city. It assumes that by discovering each other we discover ourselves.

City soul is located in the architecture of the space between people and is predicated by congruent aspirations and social commonality. Social capital, in its harmony or discord, makes or breaks a city.

Developers are generally not known for their philosophic bent, but for their market enthusiasm. But it was a developer who told me the truest thing about cities. Speaking of Florence, a place that revitalized a civilization by a standard of civic care and design excellence, my friend remarked "you know, Florence was already there, before a building ever went up."

Indeed: the soul of a city is antecedent to the construction of a city. The dream of civic communion precedes the construction of it. The civic dream stems from the desire for a city to be made happy by a common meditation on the good, enacted by a literacy of grace, in a forum where the transaction of mutual delight results in prosperity.

An ugly city speaks of a soul derogative to itself. A lovely city speaks of a people who have sought a higher version of themselves. The remedy for a city anemic to itself is to understand that vision predicates prosperity.

A healthy city recognizes a desire in the citizen that runs deeper than the utilitarian, deeper than the backwater of consumer calculation. There is in the citizen a desire for a passion that demonstrates and accelerates a keenness for life, a desire to fall in love with a city, beginning with a loyalty for what that city has been and culminating in an excitement about what it can be. We may call it a "romance" with a city; a romance that the citizen craves and labours for. When citizens recognize this, they work together to produce a great city. Not unlike the way one loves one's family, one's love infuses the civic habitat, and inspires delight.

Delight is vital to the urban romance. It is the cry of the global citizen. "Delight me in a way that will give me a reason for doing things well." When the citizen is delighted a city has a charisma of self-worth. It is what keeps generations loyal to a neighborhood; it is what entices the imagination of the global pilgrim. The charm of such citizenship is profound and seductive.

The soul of a city is about the finding of intimacy and stimulation in the streets that are a wardrobe and not just a place of business; on shorelines that lyrically address the urban; in residences that speak conviviality, under skylines that don't intimidate, but invite aspiration.

The style of delight is in the way a city looks and the way the city breathes as you watch its citizens moving with and between each other and towards each other.

The soul of the city speaks from the civic heart; and this heart must be read in terms of what it aspires to, not just in terms of acquisition. What must be heard is what the civic heart misses, not merely what the citizen has obtained. Beyond and before economy, the civic heart must be transparent. It must be read. Without reading this heart, joy will not yield itself in the civic realm. Without joy, city soul dies. The salvation of the modern city depends on the notion that a great city is not just a sustainable city, but one that justifies itself to the business of happiness.

The worst thing that can afflict a city, even in its apparent prosperity, is the deterioration of city soul. Its recovery depends on (1) seeing another citizen as a resource of sacrifice, not just as a resource; (2) using the concept of innovation as a forum of shared wonder and delight; (3) seeing the city not just as opportunities of networks, but as a gracious forum of encounter and unexpected intimacies, with gratitude for what that city has yielded.

With these elements recovered, we are guaranteed creative cities and competitive cities, because we will have cities that will have stayed human.

The task of business and governance is to enact a psychology of creativity with a credible benevolence, beyond the machinery of excitement, acquisition and entertainment. For just as there is an ecology of environment that demands more than the short-term solution, there is an ecology of the human heart that demands a faith witnessed in and by the most talented members of our society.

DIVERSITY AND THE CREATIVE AGENDA

The creative agenda miscalculates the strategies for inter-culturalism, supposing that inclusivity must lead to cohesion. But cultures are not universals. Only universals cohere. Without cohesion, the creative agenda will merely be indentured to culture and ideology. Sustainable cities must transcend cultural allegiances. The word "culture" itself may be a bogus word. It is archaic, hearkening back to a time when the term global village meant a gathering of cultures. What we have today is one global culture.

If we deconstruct the word culture, we see that it cannot mean what it once meant. It was a socio-anthropological word, devised to scientivize the human motive. It did so by the graphing of myth, ritual, common goals, beliefs, fears, and economies predicated by necessity and choice and historical vagaries. It assumed uninterrupted linear time and geo-physical parameters – unrevised by the algorithms of the virtual. After McLuhan, it is understood that media and information technology put natural cycles of time into disrepair. Meaningful rituals take place in natural time, require some homeostasis and return to a theme as musical improvisation might return to a melody.

We live in constant improvisation now, and the riffs do not settle into patterns before new ideas conscript them, forming hybridities without definable contours. Cyberspace is displacing physical space. Information technology changes our minds about ourselves before the mind settles into reflection. We are revised before we are defined. And though we may enjoy the idea of this fluidity we have become the messages of the medium. And the medium has no room for "embodied" culture. Culture as a metaphor is all we are left with.

The simulation of traditional culture is generally what passes for contemporary cultural identity. The championing of culture in the anthropological sense serves only to reassure people of a false identity; false because the originating cultural gestures are out of context in the contemporary "urban." They cannot be practiced. The set doesn't allow for growing your own vegetables in the condo. The connection to the earth amounts to a green "roof." Your religious festas will pose a security hazard to realty managers. Headdresses, Ferrari's, the clichés of cuisine and such, amount to the tradable iconographies that remind us of "cultures."

The charism of cultural diversity pleases because it flatters the sentiment of retained origin. However, origin not enacted and re-enacted, is archival. The peculiarities of group, tribal and national self that people ascribe to as cultures of origin are increasingly archival, however affectively rich they may be. What we have, in a multicultural society, is sentimentalisms that seek authentication and respect, as personal narratives seek authentication and respect. But the narratives of origin are not grist for the global consensus, much less useful for the convocation of global ideals. What we think of as the sustaining power of origin is the legitimate cry for anchored identity. It is "home" that the urban pilgrim seeks, not origin. And the task of the contemporary urban is to provide "new home." In the awakened ritual of new civic encounter, a new culture might be possible, but not by honoring the lie of sustaining origins. Origins do not sustain; they congratulate us in the confidence that comes of owning the past. They do not tell us of what we have in common besides the fables of journeying. They do not tell us of the living present, and the future where citizen must recognize citizen, without the reconfigurings of tribal styles.

WHAT DIVERSITY REALLY MEANS

In any event, diversity must be seen as larger than the ethno-racial, multicultural, or socio-cultural. It is the ideological. It is lifestyle, it is gender affiliation, it is religious. It is the political, independent of "ethnos." It is the ideation of references by which people make meaning of their lives. But meaning is more than concepts. Meaning is made up of aspirations, dreams, rejoicings, hopes, fears – elements that run deeper than a conventional study of values.

What we have on the global stage is badly neighbored belief systems, not cohering, and doubtfully negotiated by the science of cultures. Policy is stymied. Because policy deals with principles, and principles must be impelled by the eros that imagined them; they must be inspired, not in governance, but in the citizen. Principles must be felt in the exercise of empathy, where they began. Empathy is the true engine and flower of civic event, and it runs deeper than cultural values. The manufacture of empathy escapes our genius for policy. Cultures (in so far as they last) cannot negotiate; they must feel for each other. And we have no levers for this. It is only from empathy that compassion is built, and only from compassion can a passionate city evolve. The global city begins or fails here.

The citizen, discouraged from a shared forum of belief, will resort to anxieties that masquerade as political, legislative and cultural matters. In fact, that discourse conceals a primal angst in the global citizen. And that angst is the frustration of a desire – the desire to enter into "empathic citizenship" with fellow citizens.

THE CHIEF RESOURCE OF DIVERSITY

People migrate either for a better life, or for a more fortunate lifestyle; and the two are dangerously confused. Popular branding does its best say that a prosperous city is a happy one. The citizen is fooled for a while, until it is seen that the predicate of civic grace is again missing; and the cauldron of issues, rights and political populisms is stirred once more. The issues of entitlement are politically treated as commodities. Meanwhile the citizen knows full well that, to live in a global family, the "ethic of entitlement" must be replaced by the "ethic of sufficiency." It is not a market insight, but one that the market will take into account when it has come close to completely harvesting social capital. Sustainability is about the ethic of sufficiency. How can this be made attractive to the global pilgrim? It is already attractive. A shared ethos is what satiates the human spirit. Experience tells us that when the space between people is architected by a shared ethos, the errant architectures of policy and design begin to look manageable. There is in every citizen the desire to return to the currency of humanness; not the desire to subscribe to fresh principles, but to return to the narrative of the charitable and the empathic, from which the pledge of civic sacrifice is born.

This desire is the chief resource of diversity. This desire seeks to be inflamed into collective passion. More than infrastructures, more than opportunity, more than better schools, better plumbing, better business, the migrant is drawn by the lure of a shared ethos engineered by a system and peoples that see civic gladness as the lodestone of the civic experience. Before the byways and edifices, structures and over-passes, there must be the city of empathy, grace and mutuality. Equity, economy and inclusivity arrive when a city is architected by compassion.

The focus of governance must turn to the need of the citizen trying to negotiate his or her dignity in a market economy, hungry for the delight and vision and the unuttered hopes that impel migration. The goal of migration is not what it appears to be. The goal is not to "arrive." The goal is to find oneself back home again, but not by cultural markers. The goal of the voyager is to find a universality in recognizable terms. It is not an ethic of politics that the global citizen is concerned with; it is an ethic of humanity in terms that can inspire.

DIVERSITY AND MIGRATION
AND GLOBAL POLICY

Some cities have a character of civic grace that helps them withstand the uncivil. There is a natural wisdom in the civic. One notices in any city that when people get along with each other, it's because they have jumped to universals. They have the sense to know that, left to language, customs, culture and politics, they would be at each other in no time. They choose to encounter with welcome, or hostility, smile or suspicion, protocol or spontaneity, courage or fear. Policy tries to create the ambience in which the best choices are made. But the human spirit knows instinctively when it is moving either towards or away from life, towards communality or isolation, towards self-interest or civic concern. We are brought up in an age that says people must be taught these things. Marvelously, we see instances where that is not the case. Something in the spirit educates, corrects itself and acts accordingly, in spite of, and independent of, the machinations of utopian strategy.

The task for policy is to assist in the evolution of transcultural beliefs; a daunting task in a climate filled with the nagging provisos of cultural agendas and tribal entitlements. Until we have an identifiable idea of who we are as global citizens, cities will likely become provinces of the multi-nationals, nations will remain foreign and borders merely articulate our paranoia. The answer is not to be found in the industry of honoring everyone's rights – the industry that supposes that individuals and peoples have different aspirations. Behind the costumes, the politics, the agendas, the nationalities, the lifestyles, the economic apartheid, there is a hope for the universal; and the task of governance is to forge the terms for the universal. This task, once left to religion, culture, family and tribe, in a globalized world, must now fall to governance. And that task cannot be without the language of creativity.

CREATIVITY IS THE KEY TO SOCIAL COHESION

If we are to come together as different peoples in a migratory age, we must share a common ethic. It cannot be religious, political, socio-cultural or ideological. In today's diversity, such commonality is found only in creativity, common delight and shared imagination and wonder. Wonder deconstructs the stereotypes, cultural differences and tensions. The science of stitching cultures together complicates itself with every new initiative. Unless our cities cohere quickly with an inspired citizenry, variant interests and agendas will make the environment of thought despair. What bonds people to civic coherence is the common delight that creativity brings. Creativity does not mean only the arts. It means a way of thinking, being, interacting, trusting, by which the citizen sees daily enterprise in a context of adventure, allowance, mutuality, and beauty. People must emerge from heritage and lifestyles into a common forum, where their uniqueness is a given, but where their universality is defined.

Creativity works. It's a universal. It develops civic allegiance. It generates mutual trust. Municipal style, endorsing of creativity, can redress some of the damage done by a global culture of fear. Social engineering may have done its job. Human nature may have been taught to withdraw. Technology, the virtual, and an aggressive market have engineered a civic nature that will not easily encounter – that seeks to eliminate risk and outlaw the random. This alone may deprive the modern city of its destiny as a habitable place. When intimacy is suspect, a city cannot risk. A city that wishes to compete globally must claim its citizenship. And this may begin with tutoring people in the art of engaging with the random.

HOW CREATIVITY EDUCATES US TO CIVIC RISK

In a world that looks at wealth creation before it takes delight, or thinks to take delight mainly by wealth creation, risk is understood as calculated risk. In fact, radical risk is the domain of true creativity. And this introduces the art of engaging with the random.

Creativity honours the random. Allowance of the random is a mark of faith among citizens. They decide to leave what they know, for what they don't know. They depart from the safety of what they know and graduate to possibilities, as citizens sharing the creative enterprise called the city.

By permitting the random in daily encounter, one has let in the possibility of pain or joy. A sacrifice has been pledged. One has sacrificed the known to the unknown, to graduate to possibility. Sacrificing the known to the unknown is civic generousity. People recognize this as great risk and are grateful to each other. Expressed in gesturals, this is the foundation of civility. They then enjoy a premise – that there will be allowance between them, and not censure. Allowance is the great gift that one citizen makes to another. When this is publicized, it creates a climate of civility. Without this climate, there is no creative city, and no citizenship.

The allowance of the random is the mark of a city's health. Where it is evident, a city is relaxed, open to enterprise, delight and the manufacture of delight. It becomes accustomed to it, and perpetuates it.

Engagement with the random makes for courage in civic commitment. Furthermore, it teaches the citizen the art of extending oneself; for the creative enterprise is not a negotiation, a bartering of one's enthusiasms, a measured exchange of insight for insight. It is the free giving of one's energism, with faith in the reciprocal.

Faith in the reciprocal is not to be guaranteed. It is to be believed. The creative citizen seeks reciprocity, desires reciprocity, but does not wait for reciprocity. And the creative city champions this principle.

A DISCOURSE ON CIVILITY

We generally take civility to mean politeness, responsibility, care, courtesy, tolerance, respect, deference in lieu of arrogance, hospitality, an ethic of welcome, and a yielding to reciprocity. We may add to this an ethos of mutuality, common goals, and a dislike for what is aberrational to the common good. These matters appear teachable, and rationally understood. But there is nothing measured in that which inspired these notions – the human need for confluence and communion with others.

The reason for civility is in the desire for civic communion. Without this understanding civility sinks into mandate, and mere appeal to rules of order. You can't commandeer the human heart to the civic arena, without losing the sense of civility as a human revelation of possibilities.

Civility is not mere protocol or code based on agreed notions of civic order. It is not mere manners, or code of courtesy based on norms that protect the sociolect from chaos. Civil order is the offshoot of civic grace, the praxis of gratitude and response in civic event.

The word "civility" does not do justice to the genius that inspires it. Its genius is charity that comes of felt charity. Its flower is, indeed, empathic citizenship.

Civility neatly designates the outward signs of civic care and the warmth of citizenship. The eros of citizenship is founded on common love for a shared habitat. Civility is fundamentally a social strategy empowered by love.

Civic strategies make sense only in relation to the passion that inspired them. To understand this is to understand civic psychology. A city architected by the primal needs and joys of citizenry will reclaim a talent for healthy policy and city building, informed, not just by contingencies, but by intuitions that speak to the nature of citizens. And that nature seeks charity, and the exercise of charity.

THE CREATIVE MUNICIPALITY
PROMOTES CIVILITY

A city can promote and advertise the project of civility. If the market economy can accomplish consumer expectation, the municipal can underwrite social ideals. Municipal communications can lever the expectation of the civil by means of signage, publicity, ads, literature and the like. If the citizen can be reduced to feeling like a consumer, he or she can be enlivened to the volunteerism of civic care. This requires imagination, and foresight and modeling on the part of the bureaucracy, which is the actor of municipal manners. And by manners, I mean the gestures of civic grace. This requires a movement from the procedural and ritualistic, to the creative and the graceful. Civility as a collective enterprise is occasion for the public to deconstruct human encounter into its simplest elements – gratitude among citizens, sacrifice among citizens, and the delight that comes of mutuality, reciprocity and empathy. These aspects, fostered and enjoyed, make other enterprises confluent. Such is the organism of the city; that it will not take the calculation of civility as a substitute for delight.

We have for too long supposed, with liberality, that courtesy is a matter for the private citizen. It must again be seen as the necessary seduction to the public life. In an age when the private will does not easily volunteer a gregarious presence it is the duty of governance to render interpersonal engagement irresistible.

The engines for sustainability and economies require an ethical base and a respect for what motivates human encounter. Diversity will not be managed without this understanding. Nothing else will inspire collectively the negotiation of variant ideas and beliefs, if not the daily energism and delight of civil encounter.

Civility understood as an aesthetic of grace is the key to managing diversity through creativity. This civic aesthetic must be incorporated into the urban agenda.

REVERENCE AND THE CREATIVE CITY

Perhaps reverence is what we need to arrive at sustainable cities; reverence for the environment, reverence for each other, reverence for the work of city building. Maybe the "sacred" is what has been lost, thinking as we do that it is a word better suited to divinities than to the mysteries that reflect the divine. Maybe we have lost the knack of seeing each other as partners in the revelation of creation. Little wonder we act as though the enterprise were strictly our own.

Paul Woodruff

Civility stems from civic virtue. Acts of virtue, though aided by habituation, are enabled by apprehension of the good. Virtues are the praxis of spiritual intuition and spirituality begins with the apprehension of the sacred. However varied the contemporary versions of the sacred, the concept of the sacred remains universal. It is from the intuition of the sacred that all values emerge. Shared civic values depend on the shared apprehension of the sacred articulated by principles, and commonly embraced. What must be distilled from spiritualities is a common theme, to stitch together the fabric of civic care. And this cannot be done as an exercise in comparative religions.

There are two aspects to the universal apprehension of the sacred, understood as "mercy" and "compassion."

They are the central insights of all world religions and spiritualities. Virtue always refers itself to these two aspects, to their exercise and the perfecting of them.

The aspects of mercy and compassion are the core character of the sacred, the convergence point of contradicting spiritualities. Values, however driven, by whatever cultural expression, draw their meaning, or become meaningless by their proximity or estrangement from this comprehension.

Mercy and compassion are the human existential mimetic to a sympathetic universe, a cosmic benevolence, divine or otherwise. If traditional lexica offend, a vocabulary must be forged that alludes successfully to ultimate metaphors. The ultimate metaphor is beauty, which appears in the character of goodness and reasoned grace. It is the intuition of beauty that drives each citizen in the faith that makes each day possible.

The brute mandate of "respect" is meant only to enable mutual serenity under the auspices of providence. The purpose of "tolerance" is to permit variant discoveries in the light of that providence. The purpose of "equity" is to exercise the same generosity with which providence metes out its abundance. That which interferes with the felt condition of dignity under the auspices of creation falls outside of the discourse of civility. The function of civility is to elucidate that dignity in the eros of creation. We are not dignified by the peculiarities of personality, race and culture; we are dignified as common beneficiaries of a sympathetic universe, a universe that often metes out more than was expected, and often, more than is deserved. This is at the core of an understanding of civic grace. It prompts behaviour that is grateful and collaborative.

Mercy, therefore, at the heart of the civic creed, predicates the rationale for tolerance, respect, equity, and civil rights. It is justified by our experience of goodness. The reason to do good is predicated by our experience of the good.

This warrants our reverence, and reacquaints us with the concept of the sacred. To be irreverent to the civic gift by exception of tribe, blood and legacy of interest is to be subversive to the civilizing impulse. It is to be anarchical to one's self-worth and renegade to communal experience. The teleology of being human is to arrive at a higher version of oneself by the creativity of living with others.

That is why the city is seen as a sacred place, where the sacred manifests itself in the revelation of civic engagement.

The urgent task is create the terms that bind us to the sacred and at the same time point out the essential architecture of commonality. What will save the global enterprise is the tacit belief that we have one dream stemming from a universal source in the rhythm of universal aspiration. Let the terms of this aspiration be theologically free and similarly free of cultural and political leasing. We must be poets of a common metaphor. Political, ideological, theological terms will not help us mediate the fractious differences of contemporary migration and identity.

With the understanding that the reverential is founded upon mercy and compassion we then know that the reverential is at the heart of the sustainable and creative city. If these terms are not yet clear in the secular discourse, we may begin at least by evacuating our tolerance for what is inimical to mercy and compassion. It is not a moral judgement to eliminate what is ugly; it is a deference to what the beautiful commands. That which is not reverential is the enemy of the civic.

THE SPIRITUAL IN THE SECULAR

Creativity is our only language for the spirituality of the times. Shared wonder is as close as we get to communal worship. The shared humanity that art represents is the disarmament of ideology and special interest.

It is folly to attempt the universals of creativity by the parochialisms of culture. Ontology predicates culture. It is not culture that predicates ontology. The intellectual history of the twentieth century was dedicated to the subordination of "being" to culture; a fatal error, because it saw spirituality as a function of culture. Fatal, because what is awakening now in the ranks of Islam and in the reductions of Western religions is the dire and impatient need to arrive at public enthusiasms for shared ontology. The absolutes are recruiting the passions of the private citizen eager to join a public belief. The result is extremism. Extremism is not the aberration of belief; it is the containment of belief finding its release. The liberal agendas and their variant logics do not address this understanding. The global citizen seeks a consensus of faith, to touch the subterranean dreams of a global consensus.

But let us be forewarned; creativity does not clarify ontology. It offers metaphors for it. And these metaphors are windows from which the citizen glimpses the spectrum of the ineffable. And the citizen seeks to be housed in the ineffable. And that sense of cosmic hospitality is retained by a focus that uses art as a medium of the divine, and not as mere exponent of the imagination.

Creativity is not a religion. It is not even a faith. It is the faithful investigation of ultimate metaphors. In this way it can bring people to common beliefs and instruct them in thanksgiving. The imagination that offers tribute to itself deadens the experience of wonder and annihilates the creative project.

CODA

The True Ecology

And where is home? Home is not in a neighborhood, nor in a community. Home is in the unexpected welcome of the stranger. Home is in the charity reflected in the chance encounter. Home in what you want to make of the city when you are the object of kindness. Home is what you return to in the gatherings of people, in coffee shops, street corners – in those zones where you met the human eros. It might have been at a tollbooth, at a counter, in a gallery, a parking lot, in the most ridiculous or fortunate of places. The unseen city is in the happenstance – the boulevards and paths and piazzas and atriums or in the choreography of people that build a city as homage to what they have found in each other. The city is built after the architecture of care has been improvised. And the roots of it are not in the logistical or prudently designed. The roots of it are in the mystery of grace, the appetite for each other, the gusto of being curious about each other before the conventions of the visible world. It is the invisible city that is the Valhalla of the civic dream. The structure of a city is for the furthering of kindness and inter-civic munificence. We will not have livable cities until we find a reason for living in each other.

We know only that the geography of care is the true ecology and that we cannot save anything until we have saved ourselves from irreverence.

The Heart of the Creative City

Ultimately, the creative city does not look to its appearance for inspiration. It is motivated by the beautiful things it puts up or is violated by testaments to its apathy, but its inspiration comes from the civic energism of living together day by day, discovering, sacrificing together, loving together those themes and places that give them a reason to be together.

It is not an attractive city that keeps people loyal to a place and time. It is the infrastructure of mutual reliance that draws loyalty. It is the design of allegiances and affections that conduct a people to graceful movement. This is the architecture of faith that speaks more boldly than any bank tower or sports arena. The true museum is any public gathering that archives what people have gone through together and hope for together. It is not galleries that showcase a city's achievements. It is the faces of citizens, joyful and elated, boasting of the chronicle of urban life to visitors. It is not the appearance that inspires greater beauty: it is the fervor of its citizen who build a city as a tribute to what they recognize in their hearts to be a city's soul. People will make a playground of the drab, they will find respite in a brownfield, they will find repose and companioning in the abandoned and the undeveloped, because they fill public spaces with the unashamed and unabashed sentiments and glories of the human drama. But a city must have a human drama. Herein lies the secret to a creative city or town. It embraces failure, fear: connects its forays of altruism to the design of the generous, in a public confession of delight. For it knows all aspects of the mature life to be grist for common struggle and civic revelation. The human drama, the embarrassments, the satire of competition, the commanding weather of mortality, the pettiness that frames the striving heart. These are accepted, lived, shared, in a code that spites the solitary. For the solitary is the nemesis of the creative city. Anonymity is that luxury that may yet corrupt the urban future. For all our schemes of connectedness and network, for all our hopes for revitalization, it is the human drama alone that will restore our cities; more importantly, it is the unwillingness to conceal that drama that will emerge as the mark of our greatness.

THE LANGUAGE OF THE SENSES: AN AFTERWORD

CHARLES LANDRY

The city is an assault on the senses. It is a lived experience. We feel the city. It engenders emotions. It affects our psychology. Emotions drive our life, shape our possibilities, determine our reactions and our outlook on the future. Why then is the language we use to describe the city so technical, lifeless and drained of energy. It is odd that the emotional, which is a defining feature of human existence, is absent in discussions of city-making. We have lost the language of the senses....

Happily, Pier Giorgio Di Cicco recaptures the sensory, the soulfulness and soulessness of the city and puts the missing thing centre-stage: The human being.

Our language, unless we look to artists, is hollowed out, eviscerated and dry. It has little to do with people and how they feel and perceive the world. It is as if the city was just a physical container and the people were an afterthought. Urban discussion is shaped by the technical jargon of the professions, especially those in planning and the built environment. The prevalent, interchangeable words and concepts proliferating involve barren, unemotional words that are performance-driven, such as: input-output analysis, planning framework, quantitative planning goals, spatial development code, development strategy, outcome targets, site option appraisal process, stakeholder consultation, the role of the development board in delivering integrated services, income inadequacy, statutory review policy programme, neighbourhood framework delivery plan, sustainability proofing, benchmarking, underspend, empowerment, triple-bottom line, visioning, mainstreaming, worklessness, early wins, step change, livability, additionality.

No wonder civic engagement is in decline.

The language explaining how cities look is dominated by the physical without descriptions of movement, rhythm or people. This visual language comes largely from architecture and urban design and from habits of portraying classic architecture where building components are illustrated: pedestals, columns, capitals, pediments and architraves.

81

The language has broadened, yet still has a static, deadening feel. Words like space, structure, technology, materials, form, colour, light, function, efficiency and worse, by-pass, road, building. Urban design, meanwhile, sees and describes cities more as dynamic totalities: place, connections, movement, mixed uses, blocks, neighbourhoods, zones, densities, centres, peripheries, landscapes, vistas, focal points, and realms. But it all too frequently excludes the atmospherics of cities, the feeling of the look. It touches a shallow register and does not dare to be profound.

This is why you will have never read a city plan or hardly had an urban discussion that openly talks of old-fashioned words like "ugliness" or "beauty," even though we might argue what they might mean. Have you ever seen a plan that starts with the emotions or even refers to them? "Our aim is to make citizens feel enriched." "We want to create a sense of joy and passion in our city, to engender a feeling of love for your place." "We want to encourage a feeling of inspiration."

But behind the words we use there is a mind. No wonder minds that operate in a language landscape that is so detached and disembodied produce places with no soul, no connection, no feeling.

Ask yourself does the city make you shrink into yourself, make you calmly reflect, or fill you with passion? Does it close you in or open you out? Does the physical fabric make you respond with a sense of "yes" or "no"? Does it involve you? Make you want to participate? Does it help you be curious, imaginative, creative, inventive and innovative? If it does not, now is the time to act.

And whilst we are on "creativity" – the most significant argument for the "creative city" is that cities should not seek to be the most creative city in the world or region or state. They should strive to be the best and most imaginative cities for the world. This one change of word – from "in" to "for" – has dramatic implications for a city's operating dynamics. It gives city-making an ethical foundation and a value base. It helps the aim of cities becoming places of solidarity, where the relations between the individual, the group, outsiders to the city and the planet are in better alignment. These can be cities of passion and compassion.

To that end, *Municipal Mind* is a book to be grateful for.

Charles Landry is the author of *The Creative City* and *The Art of City Making*.

I would like to express my thanks to:

Charles Landry - Patricia McCarney
Cal Brook - Mayor David Miller - Elena Bird
John Campbell - Geoff Cape - Peter Kageyama
Richard Florida - Joe Lobko - Brigitte Shin
Marc Glassman - Marisa Piattelli - Shawn Micallef
Rev. Robert Nusca - Corrado Paina - Susan Serran
Eb Zeidler - Margie Zeidler - Margaret Reel
Peter Menzies - Peter Sobchak - Howard Duncan
Kip Bergstrom - Roger Garland - Ilse Treurnicht
Karen Black - Carolyn Taylor - David Soknacki
Michael Redhill - Sue Beal - Terry Nicholson
Rebecca Ward - Rui Marquez - Grace Westcott
David Harrison - Mario Romano - Bob Davis
Steven O'Bright - Stephanie Ford - Meric Gertler
Amanda Styron - Luigi Ferrara - Helen Walsh
Patrick Luciani - Alf Holden - Matt Blackett
John Bentley Mays - Joel Kotkin